When Love Flows Through Broken Hearts

Love Notes To My Children and Yours

———————

The "Amazing" Tei Street

(When Love Flows Through Broken Hearts)
Copyright © 2020 by (The "Amazing" Tei Street)

ISBN: 978-0-9770009-3-7

Printed in USA by Amazon on Demand

Dedication

This book of love notes is dedicated to one of my heartbeats; my son Christopher.

It is also dedicated to all of the mothers who choose to love their children, through the pain of a broken heart; including my mother, Theresa R. Street.

Email: amazingteistreet@gmail.com
www.amazingteistreet.com.

Foreword

"When Love Flows Through Broken Hearts" **is a compilation of prose poetry that captures the hearts of mothers or anyone rearing a child. The author of this mesmerizing easy read book exposes her own childhood challenges that parallel the roller coaster ride her son takes her on—** *for a broken heart.*

It is her written daily messages to her son that unblock arteries of anger, fear, and desperateness in hope of renewing her mother and son relationship. You feel the hurt, resentment, and sacrifice echo off the pages; but revealed between the lines in the love notes is what many mothers fear most –feelings of failure.

You see there is no easy walk to freedom anywhere—but freeing your heart will take you through the valley of heart breaks and the shadows of evil before you restore your soul and God comforts you. The greatness of the writings in this book is how one person's story heals another.

The comfort, hope and success of restoring a relationship is transpired through letters written in original format providing heart wrenching, funny, and yet truth to power language about episodes in life that many Black mothers encounter, survive and refute. The book leaves you with, 'I can relate to that… or…only if I had thought of that.'

The author, The Amazing Tei Street, is an accomplished artist. She writes with the ease as Michelangelo painted and conducts training sessions educating young scholars and those finding their way, like an award-winning actor enrapturing an audience. The "Amazing" Tei Street, mother, author and artist is someone who has allowed me to be a confidante, critic, and most of all a friend. She is someone to watch and follow.

Joyce Beatty, United States Congresswoman

Preface

On May 23 2020, in the midst of the COVID-19 pandemic, I came home to a note that rendered me breathless. After finishing the second semester of his freshman year of college with a 3.73GPA, my son Christopher decided to move out. The note he left read:

*"For a while now, I've been wanting to disappear from the world. I thought I was strong; I really did. But, I'm not. I've cut my phone off & am doing just that **Disappearing.** This has nun to do with you or us. You are perfect. I hope you don't worry. I am fine & away from the streets.*

Love,

Topher"

That was the day that my heart began to break with the passing of each day. I prayed and I cried. I cried and I prayed. And yet, my heart still yearned to have my son with me. I wasn't sure how I would get through the rest of the pandemic without knowing that he was okay and that he was safe. In the coming days he made it very clear that interaction and engagement with me was the last thing that he wanted. Though my heart was breaking, I honored his request, which was even more difficult than I had imagined it would be.

Now might be a good time to give you some context of the relationship between my son and me. Christopher is adopted; a familial adoption. As is the case with many adopted kids, he has always struggled with loving himself. The researchers say the struggle comes from the belief that if the people who were supposed to love them (birth parents) did/could not/would not, how could someone else (adoptive parent) really love them. I fully understand the internal conflict, because like Christopher, I too am the product of a familial adoption.

In the midst of a world-wide pandemic, my Son has chosen to be "in the wind," without a desire to be in communication with me. At the same time that COVID-19 was ravaging people across our nation, young, African American men were falling victim to widespread gun violence in our city. This year, our city's homicide rate would reach an all-time high. Each time I would hear of another shooting, either on the news or on social media, of a young Black male in my son's age range, I would hold my breath until they would finally release the name. Then, and only then, I would exhale...until the next shooting. Though I shared with him how much I worried about him, he was clear that he did not welcome my concern for him and refused to let me know that he was safe.

My heart was figuratively broken into a million pieces. Soon, I moved from concern to anger. I found myself praying for him, but harboring bitterness towards him at the same time. I stopped looking at his social media accounts because he was spiraling fast and furiously and indulging in behaviors that I knew would lead to jail or to the grave. I kept telling myself that I trusted God with Christopher, but deep in my mind I still worried that an early death would be his lot. For the first few nights after he left, I couldn't sleep and when I did, I tossed and turned all night. I would walk around my house practicing all of the things I would say to him if I had the chance to engage in a phone call with him. Fortunately, I did not get that chance, because it is likely that my tongue would have destroyed our relationship beyond repair. The things I wanted to say to him were not kind nor Christian. I was angry that he was cavalier about my feelings and took my love for granted. It felt as though he had no true understanding of all of the sacrifices I made for him, nor did he care. Yep, I had some words for that boy!!

On June 21st, I was going through my daily ritual of praying my begrudging prayer when God spoke to me. Yes, you heard me correctly, God spoke to me. He told me that my job as Christopher's mother is to love him; nothing else. It is not my job to critique or judge his choices, it is my job to love him through them in the same way that my Mom had loved me through the myriad of horrific choices I made during adolescence. He told me that my anger prevented me from being a true intercessor for my Son, which made him ripe for harvest by the enemy and the streets. God told me that no matter what I saw, heard or thought, I was to put my trust in Him and his ability to cover Christopher. That day, he told me to send Christopher a "love" e-card every day. I have had an online e-card membership for more than 10 years that I only used for a few birthdays a year. So, that day, as an act of faith, I sent Christopher his first card with my love note inside. Admittedly, it was pretty corny, but it was my attempt at breaking the ice. The card was a talking cheese hamburger with lettuce, tomato, ketchup, mustard on a bun. My love not to him read:

Christopher–

Hope this card isn't "buns." You were on my mind, so I thought I would reach out "Beef 4" you get your day going. I thought, "Lettuce souprise" you today. This "Must" ard be my lucky day to "Ketchup" with you. I hope this burger card isn't too "Cheesy."

Just a note to say "hello."

Love always.

~Mom

I know, I know, super lame. Don't judge me. It worked. That day he sent me a text, thanking me for the card. And he laughed. We both share the same sense of humor. From that day until this one, I have sent him an e-card with a love note from me EVERY DAY! No matter how busy or crazy my life gets, I never fail to send that card. From time to time I get a text response and he as assured me that he reads each one.

    The last six months have been filled with many highs and lows as relates to my son. Though I have opted not to view his social media, it has not stopped others from sharing pictures and post from his IG, FB and Twitter accounts with me. I am not sure why people seem to gloat at the struggle and downfall of others. Surely, they have to know that the things they share often cause me great emotional pain. I never delight in the struggles of the children of other people. I learned that from my Mom. She often said, *"I don't talk about other people's children, especially when I have children of my own. You never know what your children are capable of, out of your presence."* And, I can honestly say, I never heard her malign the children of others...EVER!

Though he has made some choices that I wish he had not, I adhered to the admonition of God. Each day, I choose to love him and not judge him. I am reminded that the thing that drew me from the streets was love. Jeremiah 31:3 reads, **"Therefore with lovingkindness I have drawn you."** The same thing that it took to draw me is the same thing I choose to offer my "Amazing" Son; lovingkindness.

On September 21st, exactly three months after I sent the first e-card, I was shocked. Christopher and I had read a book by Stephen Covey wherein he said it takes twenty-one days to form a habit. We often joked that because of our mutual ADHD we could not do anything for 21 consecutive days, so there was no danger in us ever forming a habit. My card to him that day was a little puppy that said I was thinking of him. My note to him read:

Christopher-

Do you remember that Stephen Covey says it takes 21 days to form a habit? As you know, it is hard for me to form habits, cuz my ADHD brain has a hard time focusing on any one thing for 21 days.

As a demonstration that you matter to me, note that I have not missed one day of sending you a love note since I started on June 21st. Yep, it's official, you are my habit. You are absolutely my drug of choice. :-)

I hope you are having a good day so far. Have a great week.

Love,

Mom

That day, I was talking with a friend, Alesia Gillison, sharing how much my heart aches over my son, but how much I trust that God has got him. I shared with her that I send him a love card every day, because I want him to always know that he is loved, not because of what he does, but because of who he is. I read her the card I sent that day. At that moment she said, "Tei, you have to write a book." I replied, "I already wrote a book." She told me that I should write a book about this journey of loving Christopher through my pain and his. She told me that she was sure there were other parents who were struggling with their children who could use something to give them hope. She said that other parents needed to know how to love their children through their choices.

For the next month, our conversation continued to play in my head. Then on October 27th, my son sent me a text that read, *"Thank you for showing me unconditional love each & every day. Taking time out of your morning to make sure I start my mornings on a good note. Thank you for raising me the best you could. Never really got to tell you how great of a job you did. No matter how it seems you did great. I forever love you & I'm forever thankful."*

We communicate more these days. He has reached out to ask for my advice, so that he doesn't repeat some bad decisions he made earlier this year. I don't know what tomorrow holds for us, but I do know who holds all of our tomorrows. This book is simply a compilation of the love messages I have sent to my son. I share them in the hopes that parents who have children who are struggling will gain tools for loving them until they can learn to love themselves, even while your heart is breaking. I don't pretend to have all of the answers, nor do I believe this approach is for everyone. It is just one more resource for parents until that perfect manual, "How to Raise a Perfect Child" is written. Something tells me that we might be waiting a little longer for that book. Until then, seek God and ask Him to perform surgery on your heart so that love will flow through it, even in its broken state.

DAY 2

(Talking Chinese Food Box)

Christopher-
I thought I would take a
few moments out of my day
to say hello because love is
a verb. I hope your day is
delicious and enjoyable. ☺
Love,
Mom

DAY 3

(Marching Band Card)

Good morning.

Just a note to say hello and to let you know that I am glad you are finally happy. Everyone deserves to be happy and you do too.

Love you,

Mom

DAY 4

(Pic of Him)

Dean's List Letter Comes

Christopher–

Wow!! We have come to the end of your Freshman year of college. I have to say I am both surprised and proud of how you chose to end the academic year! You are dope...when you choose to be.

As you go forward, remember what this moment feels like. When you are tempted to give in to your lesser instincts, go back to this moment and crave this feeling.

As bright as I know you are, it still shocks me sometimes when you actualize that which you are capable.

I just didn't want this day to pass without acknowledging your success. I will always be your biggest cheerleader.

Love, Mom

DAY 5

(Movie-Themed Card)

Christopher –

Life is much like the movies. There's action, adventure, drama, comedy, & horror. Just like the movies, life's emotions run the spectrum; laughter, tears, fear, excitement, anticipation, anger, and joy. It's all a part of this thing we call life. Love it... and you too!

Mom

DAY 6

(Sun Will Shine Again)

Christopher–

On days like today when the sadness of life threatens to sink me, God sends reminders that rain doesn't last always. Eventually the sun shines again.

Just know that though now may seem dark in your life, just know that God has some sunshines ahead for you too.

I hope you are having a good day. I was thinking about you and writing this note to you served as a ray of sunshine for me. Love,

Mom

DAY 7

Good morning Christopher.

This is the card that best speaks to the sentiments I want to share with you today. I know you are hard on yourself sometimes and sometimes, I am hard on you. Just because you have a bad season, doesn't mean you are not "Amazing," still.

I never forget how "Amazing" you already are, even when you doubt or forget yourself. I am here as your biggest fan and your biggest cheerleader.

Have a Wonderful Day.

Love, Mom

DAY 8

(Talking Taco Card)

Christopher–

This is nacho usual card. Shell we continue? Hope you meat today with a sense optimism. Don't let circumstances sour your mood. Lettuce us suppose that things can't get any cheesier than this card and this note. Ha. Ha.
Love, Mom

DAY 9

Christopher–

Good morning to my handsome, brilliant, kind-hearted Son. I know that during this crazy time of life, like many of your peers, you are battling your two selves. That is normal. Ultimately, the self that you feed the most is the one that will grow the most.

To love you is to know both of your selves and to choose to love the whole you. And... though I don't like some sides of you, I love you to my core.

I am praying for you and I love you Christopher. Have an "Amazing" day.

Love, Mom

DAY 10

(Pic of Us Card)

Christopher-

This pic is my favorite of the two of us. I think it best depicts how the two of us feel about each other at our core.

Today's card is simply one to tell you that above ALL else, I LOVE YOU!! Being your Mom is the hardest and BEST job/gift God has ever given me. For all that you are and are not, I am so grateful to God that YOU ARE MINE!! Love,

Mom

DAY 11

(Dog on Moped Card)

Christopher-

I thought for today's card I would send you some sunshine. I look forward to the time when COVID-19 is no more and I can take you to California where scenes like this are the norm. I can picture you on a moped riding along the beach.

Have a Wonderful Wednesday.

Love,

Mom

DAY 12

(Day After Storm Card)

Christopher–

Though it cost me $25 to talk to you yesterday, it was worth every dime. :-)

As you plan out the next few days, weeks, months and years of your life, ask yourself which life you want...and then go for it. If this street life is what you really want, stay the course you are on. If you want a different life, then change course. Either way, the decisions are yours. The beauty about adulthood is that you get to make your own decisions. The down-side to adulthood is that you get to live with the decisions that you make.

I was intrigued that I was able to figure out where you were in jail, yet your family did not. If they did figure it out, why were they absent yesterday?

At any rate, I hope you enjoy a Fantastic Friday & a Wonderful Weekend.

Love, Mom

DAY 13

Christopher-

I know you probably don't believe that I feel blessed to have and to have had you in my life. But...I do. Grandma said it best, "Being Christopher's Mom made you a better Tei. Being his Mom made you open up and share all the love that you had always been afraid to give." She was right.

Before you, I was always trying to protect my heart from being broken again. Having a biological mother who died and left me and an absent sperm donor made me doubt that anyone could really love me. Over time Grandma & Grandpa's love for me helped to heal the heart that my birth parents' absence had broken.

Each day when I pray, I pray that God will give me the strength to love you through your brokenness, until you have the strength to love yourself. I pray that my consistent love for you will do what my parents' (Grandma & Grandpa) love did for me; heal your broken heart.

When I sit down to dinner, it is lonely. When I walk past your door, I miss hearing you getting loud while playing the video game. I miss hearing the muffled whispers when you are doing dirt that you respect me too much to let me hear. :-) I miss hearing you ask me, "you good?" I miss cooking for you and watching you eat. I miss our philosophical conversations. I miss the moments when you lower your wall and let me see your heart. I even miss the nausea I feel when you walk through with the smell of weed on your clothes. LOL In summary, I miss you Christopher. I look forward to the day when God will reunite us.

Love,

Mom.

P.S.- Get some dinner on me today

DAY 14

(4th of July Card)

Christopher—

Since today is the 4th of July (a holiday I don't really celebrate, cuz we are not free), I thought I would take this time to pen you a note to remind you that no matter how far away you push yourself, you will never be out of the reach of my love for you. Time, and circumstances may change, but my love for you will persist, even after I am gone from the earth. That, Christopher is how deep my love for you flows.

I also wanted to remind you that failure is America's plan for Black people. Nothing pleases racists more than when our young people fill the jails and the graves. The KKK used to use trees and guns to kill our men. Today, they place drugs, gangs, and guns in the hands of our men and sit back and watch us kill ourselves. Don't do their dirty work for them.

There is greatness in you Son, and I will never stop praying for your success and I will NEVER cease loving you.

Enjoy your day.

Love,

Mom

DAY 15

Christopher-

I know there must be days when all you really want to do is just "Be." You don't want to carry the weight of anyone's expectations of and for you. On days like that, it is okay to just "Be."

Those who love you will love you anyway. Those who don't, they never did anyway. So, today, I am giving you permission to just "Be."

Love, Mom

DAY 16

(Bear Hug Card)

Good morning Christopher.

I just wanted to send you a hug from the heart of your Mother. Though life can be a little bananaz sometimes, never forget that you are loved...even in the midst of it all.

Love, Mom

DAY 17

Christopher-

I hope you arise on this Saturday morning and commit to having a day filled with love for yourself, purpose in your walk and joy in your soul. Those are the things I wish for you on this day.

I woke up this morning with you on my spirit so I did what I always do when you cross my mind; I prayed. I know that love and prayer are the greatest forces in the universe, so today, I just wanted you to know that I sent both forth on your behalf. Time, space, nor distance can separate you from my love. My love and my prayers will chase you down, even in the darkest recesses of your soul. So, when you are at your lowest and there is something that is still offering a glimmer of hope, just know it is my love and my prayers.

I love you Christopher.

Mom

DAY 18

Good morning my beautiful Son,
Christopher.

As usual, I woke up praying for you.
In the midst of my prayer, I
stopped to ask God for forgiveness
for the things I have done that are
displeasing to Him. Forgiveness does
not become possible until I ask for
it.

So, this morning I thought I would
ask for your forgiveness for not
always knowing what you needed.
Although I did the best that I knew
to do, I didn't always know how to
help you create a life you can love.
I know that you know I love you,
but I hope you also know that I am
clear that like all parents, I didn't

always get parenting right. As I often tell parents in my speeches. When we become parents, there are no rule books. So, most of the time, we are making it up as we go along. LOL

Today, I just want to ask for forgiveness for the times I failed you. Today, and every day, I love you.

Mom

DAY 19

Christopher-

You know how much I love sunrises and sunsets and how I am always seeking ways to capture them in photos (how many times have I asked you to the pics for me- :-)). Perhaps you don't know why I love them so much. The colors remind me that God is multi-faceted. Also, the sunset marks an ending with the promise of a new beginning and sunrise marks the honoring of God's promise that no matter how bad yesterday was, today is a new day.

You are my sunrise, because God reminds me that He has a plan for your life, no matter what yesterday looks like.

Last night when we were texting, it did not occur to me when I sent you Auntie LMC's question, you didn't know that I have not shared with anyone that you won't be returning to school. So, she was asking the question based off what you told me when we were in quarantine and you were pursuing Alpha.

I hope your today is filled with love and joy.

Love, Mom

DAY 20

Good morning Christopher.

Hitting the road in just a little bit headed back to CBus. It has been nice to just get away for a little bit from the stresses of everyday life. Feel better rested and ready to face the world again. :-)

I hope you had a great day yesterday and that your today is awesome. A couple of weeks ago, you mentioned wanting to get together. Are you still interested in getting together? If so, this weekend would work. I wanted to give it at least 14 days after you were out to make sure you don't have any symptoms.

Let me know what you think. As you are processing your next steps, just know that I am here to process with you...no judgement, just helping. As an fyi, I am always here for you. My job as your mother is to love you through your choices...and I do.

Love, Mom

DAY 21

Christopher-

Today, I just simply wanted to remind you that you are loved by me. Have an "Amazing" day.

Please let me know if you still want to get together sometime.

Love,

Mom

DAY 22

(Musical Card)

Good morning Christopher.

Just a little light music and some fun to get your day going. Hope you have a fantastic day and that you take a little time to reflect on the fact that you are still alive. For that, I am glad.

Love you Son,

Mom

DAY 23

Christopher-

I am so glad you are along on my ride of life. Does that matter to you? Do you care that I want you in my life? I know your heart hurts for a lot, but I hope your heart heals from my love for you. If I could only choose one person (other than my Mom) to be on the ride of life with me, you would be my one.

Let's choose each other.

Love, Mom

DAY 24

Christopher-

Though today is gloomy and rainy outside, I wanted to send just a little sunshine today. It is a great reminder that you are my sunshine. :-)

Today, no matter what the day brings, keep in mind that there is an old, Black, fat lady sitting on the NW side of town, praying for you and giving thanks to God for you. Today, I will focus on the blessing of life. These days as Grandma get worse, I hang on to good memories to keep me from falling apart. I was over there on Thursday and she asked me where you are and why you don't come to see her. I just said, "I don't know Mom. He'll come see you." Make some time this week to go see her please. Grandpa asks about you all the time. They are not getting young Son. You don't want any regrets.

Well, I'm getting ready to make me some breakfast before I watch church on tv. :-) I hope you have a great Sunday. Have some Sunday dinner on me.

Love,

Mom

DAY 25

Christopher-

Today is a great day to press restart and to begin again. As long as you have breath in your body, you have an opportunity to reinvent yourself. Only you can determine and define who you are, who you want to be and how you want to walk in the world.

Each day, I rise and make a conscious decision to be the best version of myself today. I am a better person each day, not because I simply want to be, but really because I work to be.

I hope that today meets you with lots of hope, happiness and a desire for a Jeremiah 29:11 experience.

Love,

Mom

DAY 26

Good morning Christopher.

CONGRATULATIONS!! You made it through another day and into a new day. As bullets and bodies drop all across Columbus, making it to a new day is cause for celebration.

On a serious note, I just wanted to send an upbeat card and message to you today. I am convinced that today is going to be a Terrific Tuesday for us. I hope that you find something to do today that brings you joy.

I love you with my whole heart.

Mom

DAY 27

Good Morning Christopher.

Just a note to let you know you are in my thoughts and my heart this morning...and every morning.

As more and more bodies drop across the city, my prayers are greater and greater for your covering. I trust God, but don't be a fool and make unwise decisions. Lay low.

I love you to pieces. You promised to let me know every day that you are safe. I have not heard from you in days. Are you good? Love you much!! Mom

DAY 28

Good morning Christopher. Just a little humor mixed in with truth to start your day.

As I prepare to join Kenny, Uncle Andre and the rest of the Alphas for the African American Male Wellness Walk, I get excited at the thought that one day, we will all be reunited and we will take a complete Fam Pic with you in it. No matter what is happening right now, I trust God for what is to come. I don't think your current condition will be your forever condition.

I love you and will be thinking about you as I walk for the health, including the mental health, of all the men in my life that I love.

Love you much and don't forget to have Tim & Amy call me while he is checking out your car.

Love,

Mom

DAY 29

Christopher-

This morning during my prayer, I was giving God thanks for the gift of you and Kenny as my Sons. So, I thought it ironic when I saw this card. I decided this card is the one for today.

I know you have a hard time believing that God has a good and perfect purpose for you life, but I have enough faith for the both of us. I know you don't usually feel great about who you are, so it is hard to believe that someone would view you as a "gift." But, for me, loving you makes me complete. It lifts me and it strengthens me. It isn't always easy, but as my capacity for love grows, I realize the gift of you make that capacity for growth possible.

Thank you for being part of my "Why!" Don't give up on you. Fight your way back to yourself. You are worth it!!

Have a great Sunday.

Love,

Mom

DAY 30

Christopher-
Just wanted to start your week
off with a humorous ecard. But
on a serious note, I am deeply
grateful to God that given the
heat of our streets, I did not get
THE call from the police or the
coroner this weekend. I am
praying for you! I love you and if
you are ever looking for a route
out of the life you are living, I
am here.
My love for you will never cease.
The Bible says that even if I die,
my prayers for you will go on in
the earth. Be safe and let me
know you are good.
All of my love,
Mom

DAY 31

Christopher-

This morning, after a VERY long day yesterday, I awakened feeling extremely happy and hopeful. I hope your day is filled with so much happiness that you too will want to dance. I thought about you and literally felt like dancing.

Google the song, "I Hope You Dance." Listen to/Read the lyrics. Some of them say, "and when you get a chance to sit it out or dance, I hope you dance." I do Son.

Love, Mom

DAY 32

Christopher-

I am so glad I don't need a special occasion to let you know that you are special. I hope as each day passes you become more and more aware of all the things that make you special. When I see you I see beauty, brains, and brilliance in one solid package. Yep, to me you are special not because of anything that you have done, but just because you are you.

Have a wonderful Saturday!! I love you Christopher.

Mom

DAY 33

Christopher-

Today is a great day to smile. Whether you are having a good day or not, smiling changes the atmosphere. I hope you have reasons to smile today. Thinking about my baby today is making me smile.

Love,

Mom

DAY 34

Christopher-

Today, I just want you to be abundantly clear that today and always, I got your back!!

I guess you posted your mug shot and said you are this way cuz nobody showed you love. I know it is a song. I was asked how I feel that that is the narrative you want people to believe.

I told him that I don't follow you on social media because when I did it made me crazy and that at this time in my life, I seek peace, so I have not seen it. I told him that if that is what you posted, you and I know the truth. I don't live my life for what kids think on IG. I don't have any feeling about it, because most of your new life is manufactured. And, if you know nothing else, you know that at one somebody showed you love.

I love you yesterday, today, tomorrow and until I take my last breath.

Love,

Mom

DAY 35

Christopher-

I saw this card this morning
and thought of you. You know
how much I love sunrises and
sunsets. I love beautiful skies
because they remind me of the
greatness of God. Your
existence in my life also
reminds me of the greatness of
God.

Today, I hope you take time to
embrace that unlike some, you
have been given another day of
life. This means one more day
to experience this thing we call
life. I am sure many who left
us young and too soon would

give anything to have another
day to get life right.

I love you and as always, I am
praying for you.

Love,

Mom

DAY 36

Christopher-

I didn't say it, the card did. LOL Psych...for real though, I love you. If you were not on the planet, who would miss you...I would. I often wonder that myself. Would you miss me? Well, someday I will die. You have an opportunity to not miss me now. Will you take it?

Let's connect...SOON!!!

Love,

Mom

DAY 37

Christopher-

When I heard this song and the sentiments it expressed, it made me smile. I hope it makes you smile too.

When I think about all the fake trappings of the world, it makes me appreciate the things that really matter; Faith, Framily (friends & family) & fruitfulness. I can honestly say that none of the material things of the world will ever matter as much to me as you and Kenny. I don't need anything but the two of you to make my life complete. Those things are nice, but they can never fill the voids left by broken relationships.

If you ever decided that you need me as much as I need you and that you love me as much as I love you, I will be here for you.

Love,

Mom

DAY 38

Christopher-

I don't know why I love you so much, but I do. Even if you NEVER decide to engage with me again, you will always know that I love you. Have an "amazing" Saturday.

Love,

Mom

DAY 39

Christopher-

Uncle Andre and I were just talking about you and your cousins. I shared with him how much I love his boys and that my heart hurts that one has been in jail since January. He didn't have anyone to post bail for him, so he is in jail in West Virginia, still waiting on his court day. The other is back and forth between here and West Virginia trying to make $$ selling weed. And you are out in the streets trying to find yourself. None of you are where you really want to be in life, but none of you know how to get your lives back on track.

I wanted to tell you what I told Uncle Andre. I love you in spite of yourself. I pray every day that you don't get so far out there that there is not path back to a good life. Just know, when you are ready to get back on track, I'm here.

Love,

Mom

DAY 40

Christopher-

I know that when life is tough it seems like everything is caving in on your head. Rest assured that it is only a season and it will pass.

I know that my tough stances sometimes makes you angry, but you know that my love does not cease, even in those moments.

Handling business before fun is an important lesson. The comment you made "like I just got to choose when I start," made me know you lack drive.

There are temp agencies where you could have worked this week until you start the actual job. That would have produced a paycheck that would have allowed you to pay your phone bill. You have known since last month that you had a bill. You could have sent me $22.75 each week when you got your unemployment check. You didn't do that. You told me last month that you would not stiff me on the bill if I kept you on my account. You cannot pay bills when you feel like it Son. You don't even call me on the phone that I paid for last month and you want me to extend you grace? If you had your own account and did not pay the bill, they would cut off the service until you paid it.

What bothered me more than you not having the funds is that if I hadn't texted to ask about it, you were not going to bring it up. At no point did you reach out to talk to me about covering you until you get the money.

As I close this card, I do so still loving you. A phone bill will not change that. I do love you very much Christopher.

Mom

DAY 41

Christopher-

Man...There's so much I could write in this card, but no amount of words could accurately capture the depths of my love for you. Whether you are upstairs, across town, or across the country, my love would still seek you out. There is not space or place (not even death) that can diminish my love for you.

As you navigate the world, just know that the compass you need for decision-making is already inside you. God gave you a conscience and I gave you good decision-making tools so that when you are out there in the world, you will not be consumed.

The passing of Kendall's Dad caused me to think about my own mortality. I wondered if I died if you and Kenny would be secure in the knowledge that though my love isn't perfect, it is deep and it is sincere. I wondered if the two of you would find solace/comfort in knowing that by me, you were loved. I wondered if you would have all of the skills and knowledge you needed to make a great place for yourself in the world. I wondered, if you would be okay.

As life comes at your fast, stop, take a breath and ask yourself, "will the decision I am about to make, impact my life for the better now and long-term?" If the answer is "YES," then go for it. You are equipped. Heal the parts of your heart that are broken so that you will have a whole heart with which to love growing forward, Son.

You are a good man, who sometimes makes bad decisions. The totality of the measure of your manhood is not based soley on the poor choices. It also takes into account the good choices too. None of us is all bad or all good. Your choices sometimes make me sad, because I know they have short and long term implications for you. But, they don't diminish or cease my love for you. The Bible reads, "Faith, Hope, & Love, these three, but the greatest of these is love." I Corinthians 13:13

Have a magnificent Monday my "Amazing" Son.

Love,

Mom

DAY 42

Christopher-

Yesterday was a great day.
Hearing your voice made my
heart glad. Auntie Dionne had
tears in her eyes cuz it has
been forever since she has seen
or heard you.

Hearing your voice reminded me
how much my heart loves you.
That was a gift. Thank you for
being receptive to my counsel.
I hope you know that all I ever
want for you is life's BEST. I
hope you know that the reason
God made me your Mom is
because He knew you would
need someone who messed up as

much as you have. He knew you would need someone who understood and who would not judge you, but would help and love you through this crisis of your life. God knew that I would offer you the kind of love that I needed when I was a messed up 19 year old. He knew that you would need loving guidance whose voice was stronger than the voices of chaos in your life.

God also knew that I would need a Son who loves me and will get his life together so that he can be here for me too. He knew that I would need you as much as you need me. He knew that I would need a

Son who would be my hero...I know you will be that for me.

I am just so grateful that God knew we needed each other.

Love, Mom

DAY 43

Christopher-

I thought you would find this card adequately corny and funny, so I decided to start our week out on a funny note. Yep, your laugh is one of the things I miss most about you. I miss hearing you trying to find 100 ways to get me to say "What," so you can say "Chicken Butt." Bwaaaahhh. I'm still too good.

I hope your week is off to a great start and that you are getting yourself ready to start working this week. I hope you have a fantastic day filled with joy, love and peace.

All my love, Mom

DAY 44

Christopher-

There is seemingly no end to my cornyness. But, you wouldn't have it any other way.

As I have been processing the death of Chadwick Boseman, like many people, lots of thoughts have flooded my mine. One thought I cannot shake is about his circle. He had cancer for 4 year and not one person in his circle EVER told a soul. He made 7 movies while battling cancer. His friends held his secret, while cheering him on to reach his goals. We all need friends like that.

As you are evaluating your life in the next month, be quiet and be still. Say little, listen and watch much. ANYONE who cheers you further from your goals and closer to your destruction should be 'Sus. Anyone who steers and cheers you towards those things that will enhance or better your life should be squad. Learn to discern the difference.

All my love,

Mom

DAY 45

Christopher-

I just wanted to take a moment this morning to say Congratulations on starting your new job. I hope that you like it and that it will help you to feel purposeful for a while. I hope that it helps you distinguish between a job and a career. Do your best and make the employers wonder why you are in this position, because you are so smart, talented & skilled. That happened to me and it launched my career.

I have a full day, but I will be praying for you, as I always do. I love you more than you will ever know.

Mom

DAY 46

Christopher–

I just wanted to reach out to encourage you to be safe this weekend. They are predicting a violent weekend here in Cbus and I just want to make sure my baby is safe.

Also, Aunt Tanya is hosting us at her new place on Monday at 3:00. She told me to make sure I invite you. If you plan to come, I am happy to send you the address. I will also be happy to pick you up at a designated location if that works. We will have Uncle

Skip's ribs, burgers, corn on the cob and other stuff too.

I love you and I know everyone would love to see you. Let me know what you want to do...don't not respond. :-)
Love, Mom

DAY 47

Christopher-

I just wanted to reach out to encourage you to be safe this weekend. They are predicting a violent weekend here in Cbus and I just want to make sure my baby is safe.

Also, Aunt Tanya is hosting us at her new place on Monday at 3:00. She told me to make sure I invite you. If you plan to come, I am happy to send you the address. I will also be happy to pick you up at a designated location if that works. We will have Uncle

Skip's ribs, burgers, corn on the cob and other stuff too.

I love you and I know everyone would love to see you. Let me know what you want to do...don't not respond. :-)

Love,

Mom

DAY 48

Christopher-

Good afternoon Son. This card is so late because, I wasn't feeling well, so I slept in. But, when I awoke you were on my mind and I just wanted to remind you that no matter how you see yourself or how others see you, I, as your Mother, see you as a gift from God.

I know that the pitfalls of life can have you thinking that you are not worth much, but in those times just remember that God thinks you are "amazing" and so do I. That doesn't mean you don't have not so great sides to you, but it does mean that your good far outweighs your bad.

I hope your Saturday is awesome.

Love,

Mom

DAY 49

Christopher-

Today, I just wanted to send you a message of hope. Your best days are still in front of you. God will restore all that you have allowed the enemy to steal. He is a restorer.

No matter what you are going through, don't lose hope that better days are ahead. God loves you and so do I. He wants what is best for you. When you feel torn when making poor choices, that is God telling you that He loves you and wants you to choose well.

I pray your Sunday is awesome.
All of my love is released to
you today.

Love,

Mom

DAY 50

Christopher-

Just a love note on this Labor Day to wish you a great day of celebration. I had hoped you would opt to join us, but since you didn't respond to the invite, I'll just assume you are not interested in spending today with us.

Whatever you are doing, I hope it is fun and filled with love.

Love,

Mom

DAY 51

Christopher–

Good morning to my "Amazing" Son. Today is the first day of school, so as you can probably imagine, it is a very busy day for me. But, I still wanted to come on to just let you know that I love you.

Last night, it occurred to me that you NEVER respond to my requests to get together with me or with my family. I apologize that I have not taken the hint that this daily card and occasional text from you is the extent of the relationship that you want with me and us.

Going forward, I will still send you these cards, because I always want you to know you are loved. I don't however want to keep pushing for a relationship that you no longer desire. You have a right to choose who you have in your life and who you don't. I am sorry that it took me this long to get the clue, because you didn't want to just come out and say it. Please forgive me. Perhaps it was just my heart hoping we could still have a relationship. At any rate, I promise to stop pushing for connection.

I do love you immensely and I hope that you will continue to

let me know that you are safe
so I don't worry.

Have a great day, and contact
or no contact, you are LOVED.

Love,

Me

DAY 52

Christopher-

Just a really quick message to remind you that nothing you have done disqualifies you from my love, or God's love. Both are unconditional. You don't have to do or be anything to earn it.

I love you.

Mom

DAY 53

Christopher-

Today, I just wanted to wish you joy and peace. I hope that you are engaging yourself in things that bring you joy. Happiness is fleeting and surface, but joy goes down in our souls.

I hope the weekend is filled with good things and that I find you safe on the other side of it Monday.

Love,

Mom

DAY 54

Christopher-

On this Saturday, I simply hope that life gets better for you. I am sending rays of light and love to you in the hopes that it will brighten your day.

I am not really sure there is anything I can say or do to make a positive difference in your life, so, I will simply cling to the hope that you know you are loved because of and in spite of who you are and how you show up in the world.

Love,

Me

DAY 55

Christopher-

Have had an "amazing" weekend with lots of fun and lots of great reflections. Last night, while sitting by the water with friends, just kickin' it, I had some revelations that were freeing for me. I thought I would share a few with you, though, not all of my revelations were about me and you. Here we go:

1. Real love doesn't require you to do anything to receive that love. You just have to be.

2. I am not responsible for your choices. I was responsible for

teaching you right from wrong and once I did that, the choices you make are your own. So, I don't have to feel bad or guilty for those choices.

3. It is okay to know your choices and love you in those choices and through those choices.

4. I love you and the evidence they would use to convict me is that in spite of everything you have done and continue to do, my love for you is never ending.

Hope you have an "Amazing" Sunday.

Love, Me

DAY 56

Christopher-

My love for you is a 24/7/365 Affair. Never forget that.
Love is stronger that any force on earth. God designed love to be the strongest force. My love WILL win out.

Have a magnificent Monday.

All my love,

Mom

DAY 57

Christopher-

If your depression is anything like mine, as my mind starts to contemplate a change in seasons, my depression tries to kick in. If that is happening for you, dig deep and seek the things that give you light and hope.

I just wanted to tell you today and everyday that you are in my thoughts and prayers. You are never too far from God for him to reach you. He loves you. He wants a relationship with you. The challenge is that He consistently tells us that we can't serve two masters. You can't serve him and satan at the same time. God will let you have what you want, because He believes in free will. When you serve two masters, you are never happy because there will always be internal conflict.

Part of the reason you resist a relationship with me so much is because I am a reminder of the good that God has placed in you and in your life. You can't be comfortable living the way that you do in my presence, because you know what the good side of life looks like. So, the conflict forces you to choose. I don't force you to choose, the internal conflict does. Your love for me (except when you are angry and tyring to hurt me) won't allow you to let me see you all tatted up with your grill. That's why the pic you sent me was head on and no smile. I appreciate that respect Son. But, just know, it isn't necessary to hide. I have known forever, and still it has not changed my love for you. It's your life, and I don't have to live with your choices. I just have to love you through them. And I do.

Have a great day Son.

Love, Mom

DAY 58

Christopher-

It is just becoming light outside as I type this card. I chose this card because the brightness of it made my spirit happy. I hope that when you open, it will brighten your day too.

It is a great reminder that in our darkest times, God is a light unto our path. As much as I love you, this is a reminder that God loves you far more.

Love,

Mom

DAY 59

Christopher–

Today is a great day to love on yourself and to give yourself grace for your journey. You have made mistakes. So what? Forgive yourself. We have ALL made mistakes. God does not hold you captive to your mistakes. Ask God for forgiveness and make a different choice next time.

Today is a great day to love those around you because tomorrow is promised to no one. Today, I choose to love you with every fiber of my being. Go be great!!

Love, Mom

DAY 60

Christopher–

I thought I would send you into the weekend with little laughter and light-heartedness.

I know life has had you going long and wide lately, but rest assured, you have what it takes to bust up the craziness that life throws your way. You are fast and your vertical is 30", so I have no down, you will intercept the craziness and run like the wind to score at the end of the day.

I pray you are having a good week. If not, I pray it gets

better and that you have a great weekend. No matter what, I am here for you and I've got your back. Fyi...I put a little $$ aside if you decide to go back to school.

Love,

Mom

DAY 61

Christopher-

Man, it has been a busy day. Had EMBODI kickoff today, then lunch with Auntie Baby Sands, then the drive-in concert tonight. Just got home and realized that I did not send your card today.

I hope you are having a great weekend and that things are turning around for you. I dare you to reach for greatness. No matter what, I love you.

Mom

DAY 62

(Big Announcement Card)

Drumroll...

Christopher-

YOU ARE LOVED. THAT IS ALL. :-) THAT IS ENOUGH.

Use this B-Dubs gift card to have dinner on me.

Love,

Mom

DAY 63

Christopher-

Welcome to another day that God has made and blessed you to see. I pray your week is off to a great start.

Since you have shared anything about your job, I am assuming you decided not to work. I hope that is not the case, but again, that is your decision.

Today's message is one to encourage you not to give up on you. I have not given up on you. I believe that the greatness that is in you is far bigger than those things that are not so great. We all have goodness and evil inside of us. We get to control which will be greater. Whatever we feed, grows. I used to believe that there was more evil in me than good and one day I realized that was because I expended more energy on those things in me that were negative. When I stopped feeding the messages in my head a constant diet of negativity, and filled my head with positivity instead, my life began to change.

I hope you are questioning anyone who doesn't want the goodness in you to win. Are they really your "Bros" & your "Fam?"

I love the whole of who you are.

Mom

DAY 64

Christopher–

Good morning. As fall is upon us, it is always a reminder that Winter is coming. Like you, Winter is always a hard season as the days have less sunlight, more hours of darkness, cold (which we both hate), the need to wear more clothes (which we both hate), and the onset of higher levels of depression (which we both have). I hope that when those days come, you will go back, open some of the sunshine filled cards I have sent you and be inspired.

I am most inspired when I reflect on God's love for me, that I clearly don't deserve (grace & mercy), and the love of the people that I call family who wrap me up and protect me from the harshness of the world. I hope that when you feel down, you too will reflect on God's love for you and on the love that I have for you that comes without strings.

There will always be times where we don't agree with each other, but for me, those times don't necessitate me ceasing love for you. Even when I am upset at you, it is your actions that I deplore, not you. You are one of the lights of my life. Every day, I begin my prayers with you on my lips to God. Every night, I end my day with you on my lips with prayers to God for your covering. We don't have to agree to love.

My love for you will go on in the earth, long after I am gone from the earh.

All of my love on this Wonderful Wednesday.

Mom

DAY 65

Christopher-

Yesterday, as we learned, yet again, that there is no justice for Black people in America, naturally, my thoughts went to you and Kenny. I thought, "what more should I be doing to ensure the world is better for my 2 Black sons?"

As a Black woman, I felt great pain because nobody loves us or appreciates the historic and contemporary sacrifices we have made to ensure the continued existence of our race. For 401 years on this continent, we have survived the rape by white men, *the abuse of white women, and the disrespect and disregard of Black men. And yet, we are still standing.*

Usually, all of the focus of our racial justice movement is focused on the killing of Black men, so mourning the lack of justice for a Black woman feels weird.

If I could give young Black men two messages, I would say:

1. Love Black women like we love y'all.

2. Stop aiding the police & white people in the annihilation of Black people.

All of my love,

Mom.

DAY 66

(Dog on Moped at Beach)

Christopher-

This card made me smile and made me long for some California time. One day, I hope you can join me on one of those trips. I really think you would love California.

This is going to be a beautiful weekend, so I hope you avail yourself and enjoy!! Whatever you do, be safe.

Love,

Mom

DAY 67

Christopher-

Today's message is simply thank you for the call yesterday. I appreciated it.

Today, I hope that in between puffs (LOL) you will take the opportunity to inhale some of the good things life has to offer. You don't want to look back and see that you spent so much of your life in a fog, that it passed you by. As you know, time waits for no man and it passes quickly.

Enjoy your day. If you are gonna smoke, go outside, walk in the woods and take in the world while you do. Oh, don't get caught though. :-) Love you much, Mom.

DAY 68

Christopher–

Just a note to say Hi and I love you. I am headed to meet friends and family to walk to end Alzheimer's. As you know this is deeply personal to me. This is my 4th year doing it. This year, my team raised over $800 to go the Alzheimer's Association.

Have an "Amazing" day.

Love,

Mom

DAY 69

(Day after he stood me up for my Birthday)

Christopher–

Happy, Happy Monday. I hope today is the beginning of a great week of happiness and joy.

As you go through this week, I hope it brings you one step closer to your dreams. Never forget that God is a dream maker and can bring you the good desires of your heart. I pray that you never stop dreaming about a better life.

Have a great day and an even greater week.

Love,

Mom

DAY 70

Christopher-

Great morning to you. My prayer today is that you might feel the immense love that God has for you. Nothing you have done disqualifies you from his love. He sees all, hears all and loves you still.

Of course, I also want to take the opportunity to reiterate my great love for you. I pray that even when your mind is playing tricks on you, your heart speaks this truth to you; you are abundantly love.

Enjoy this beautiful fall day.

Love, Mom

DAY 71

Christopher-

"When things go wrong, as they
sometimes will

When the road you're trudging
seems all uphill,

When the funds are low and
the debts are high

And you want to smile, but you
have to sigh.

When care is pressing you down
a bit...

REST IF YOU MUST, BUT
DON'T YOU QUIT!"

This is an excerpt from the
poem, "Don't Quit" that you

would have learned this fall on line for Alpha. Just as everything you do on line is applicable to some facet of life, this poem is especially applicable for your life in this moment, having nothing to do with school or pledging.

As you struggle from day to day, don't quit! Live to fight another day. In spite of how hard you are fighting to die, God has greater plans for you to live. All of what you are going through will be for God's glory when He delivers you and you tell your story. I believe God's promises to me for your life. No matter what you want me to believe, I don't trust me or you. I do however, trust God. I know He still has big plans for you. Even if I am not alive to see them, I know you are going to be great some day!!

I pray every day that you will stop hating yourself so that you can find enough strength to just love yourself back to wellness. Just know that even in the midst of all of the craziness, chaos and white noise, I am pushing past it all to continue loving the man that I raised.

My love is unconditional and unfailing. Even when you don't love me back, it does not impact my love for you. I love you to life; this one and the next.

Have a Thankful Thursday Son.

All my love,

Mom

DAY 72

Christopher—

Today, as I begin the weekend, I wanted to tell you how much I adore you. My new tattoo that I am getting this weekend is of a Black Panther with red eyes. The Black Panther symbolizes loyalty, strength, endurance, diligence and ingenuity. The red eyes represent the fire that burns inside. As I chose this animal, I couldn't help but think how those are also the traits that are part of you as well. Those are the best parts of you. I hope you don't forget that.

I hope you have a fantastic weekend. Do something good for you. Love, Mom

DAY 73

Christopher—

Good Saturday afternoon, Son. I just wanted to come on to wish you a Happy, Happy Saturday!! I pray your day is filled with God's blessings.

Last night we gathered at Kenny's for dinner to celebrate his brother Malcolm's promotion on his job. Kenny surprised us with the great news that he is being promoted to Lieutenant Colonel.

All (me, Kenny, Malcolm, and both their Moms) remarked that the only thing that would have made it the celebration better would have been having you present. So, you were missed.

I love you Christopher. Mom

DAY 74

Christopher–

The fall is upon us. It is a season of change and a great time to pivot one's life. I hope you use this time to think about the changes you want to see in your life and the plan you can craft to make the changes happen.

I hope your Sunday is super dope.

Love,

Mom

DAY 75

Christopher-

Early this morning, (4am), I got a call from the Mother of a young many who was murdered. I did not know her, but she just needed someone to pray for her and to give her a motivational word.

After getting my head together being awakened abruptly, I did pray for her and tried to offer her words of comfort. But really I just listened. She was inconsolable as she tried to process the grief of lossing her son to gun violence here in CBus. I didn't really know what *to say to her. So, I just listened. The pain in her voice was piercing. It made my heart ache.*

After hearing her, I prayed to God, that I will never know that kind of pain. I know you don't really think of me as your Mom, but, I know given my love for you, that kind of pain would be unbearable. Even your bio-Mom doesn't deserve this kind of pain. I pray neither of us ever has to feel this. And for what, so fake ninjas in the street can give you fake "ooo's & aahs" in life and wear fake R.I.P. shirts with your pic on it in death?

I love you more than you could possibly entertain in your mind. Burying you would devastate me. I just had a thought...maybe that's your goal.??? But at any rate, I love you tooo much to lose you to the streets. So, my war against the devil for your soul, just intensified.

Stay safe Son and know that no matter what, I have entrusted your life to God and I trust Him!!!

Love,

Mom

DAY 76

Christopher-

As I am watching the sun rise, I am thinking about the sunshine you have brougth to my life. Much of what I loved about the past few years of my life are things that would not have been possible had you not been in my life; football games, crazy Christmases, track meets, laughter in my house, connections to other parents, moments to teach values and feelings of love in my heart. For those things, I simply say, "Thank You." That is enough to smile about today. In fact, as I type this, I am smiling.

I hope you are being loved (loved, not sexed...LOL) at this time of your life. I hope those in your life know that you area treasure and a gift. I hope they love you, not because of anything you do, but simply because you are. You deserve that.

I love you still...and always.

Mom

DAY 77

Christopher-

I pray that you are well. I pray that God is infusing you with His love and care. I pray that God covers you each and every day until you come back to yourself. I pray that you will always know that in you is a giant slayer waiting to rise up and slay the giants that seem to consume you. I pray that when you are on the mountains, you will be surrounded by people deserving to be there with you and that when you are in the valleys, those are the same people surrounding you. It is in the valleys of life that you know who your real friends are. If they are real friends you will know because they will appeal to your best self and not your worst. If that is not the case, give them side eye.

I pray that in the midst of all of your life, you wlll always know that you are loved, unconditionally. I pray that you will always know that you don't have to clean up your life to be loved by me. You simply have to exist. Each morning I rise praying for you and I go to bed, praying for you. You have given me a more consistent prayer life and for that, I am grateful.

Today, my beautiful Son, rest in the knowledge that God has got you, cuz I have His ear. :-)

Love, Mom

DAY 78

Christopher-

This morning, I have been up since 4:00am preparing for my colonoscopy today. Early morning gives ways to honest prayers and heartfelt thoughts; this morning both led to you. I pray you feel the magnitude of my love each day as I pour out my heart on the canvas of these cards. I hope that when you are feeling great, these cards inspire you even more. And I open that when you are feeling low, you go back, read a couple and rest in the knowledge that you are abundantly loved. And in those moments I hope you smile.

Today is Uncle Andre's Birthday. I am sure a text from you would make his day. I am taking him out for lunch after I have this procedure done.

All my love, as always,

Mom

DAY 79

Christopher -

This morning, I heard your voice and I thought you were in the house. I said, "you good Son." You didn't answer and I got nervous. Then, I woke up.

It was so good to hear your voice. Though it was only a dream, I knew it was God reassuring me that He has got you. That thought, that God has got you, gives me more peace than you will ever know.

I am so grateful to God for your life. You are so special. I can't wait til the day when you can see how awesome you really are. Until that day, I will believe for both of us.

I hope you have a day filled with love. Know that from 1324 is nothing but love.

Love,

Mom

DAY 80

Christopher–

Today was filled with DELTA from 7:45am - 5:30pm. So, I am just getting free to send my love card to you. You are so much a part of my daily thoughts. My thoughts today were about how much I love your laugh. When you get tickled, it makes my spirit happy. Yesterday's text about the expenses gave me life.

I hope you are having a great weekend. Enjoy your evening.

Love you with my whole heart.

Mom

DAY 81

Christopher-

This morning as I watching church on tv, I have you forefront in my heart and mind. Though the angels that God has dispatched to watch over you, likely don't look like those in this e-card, I am nonetheless convinced that God has, on my behalf, dispatched His angels to watch over you. Today, my prayer is for a healing of your mind, because until that is healed, the healing of your heart is not possible. One of the things I do is keep my mind affixed on images of

you that reflect who you really
are. Those images are a great
reminder of what God has
promised me concerning you.

Faith is not about those things
we can see. Faith is actually
about those things we cannot.
My faith rests in God who can
do ANYTHING. I am proof of
that. So, today, no matter
what the enemy wants me to
see, I will continue to block out
any images that don't reflect
who God says you are. It is
through those lenses that I
choose to see you, Son.

Today, I declare that you
WILL walk out the purpose for
which God created you. I love
you my second born Son. Like

your brother, you did not grow under my heart, but you definitely grew in it. I love you, Christopher.

Mom

DAY 82

Christopher-

So, I am starting a new podcast for Black Mothers. I have been receiving questions from Black Mothers from across the country that I intend to use as the basis for the podcast. Last night as I was reading through questions with my producer the one question that stood out to me is the inspiration for todays Love Note to you.

What are the things your child(ren) know without a dbout about you? Here's 10 things I think you and Kenny know about me. Am I right? :-)

1. I LOVE God!!

2. I am down for my Sons like 4 flat tires.

3. #FOE for me; Blood (if I mess with you) & Chosen (cuz I mess with you).

4. If I love you, I ride with AND for you.

5. I don't have to agree with you to love you.

6. I would kill a ninja over my Sons and sit in jail singing hymns.

7. I don't stay angry long.

8. I have a bad temper.

9. I pray for my Sons every day.

10. Even when they mess up, I still show up, cuz Love is a Verb!!

Which ones do you agree with?

Love,

Mom

DAY 83

Christopher-

My beautifully handsome Son- I just thought today Tuesday-rific day to just say "Hi." I hope you never take for granted that someone is thinking about you and taking time to let you that YOU MATTER. Yes, ALL Black Lives Matter, but YOUR Black Life Matters to me.

Be Blessed today Son and enjoy one of the few beautiful days we have left.

Love,

Mom

DAY 84

Christopher-

I just thought this card was funny. But the sentiments are mine nonetheless. I love you in more ways than I can count and I just thought Wednesday was a great day to just remind you how wonderful I think you really are.

Keep pressing through to the other side, because that is where your best lies.

Have a Wonderful Wednesday, Son.

Love,

Mom

DAY 85

Christopher-

It's supposed to rain today,
bringing forward the first real
signs that Fall is coming. As
much as I love the rain, I know
that sometimes, for some
people, it brings with it a little
gloominess.

I wanted to send this particular
card today to remind you that
on your darkest days, the ray
of love coming from your
Mother's heart is bright enough
to drive back the darkest
clouds, if you let it. I can't
help it, but everytime you pop
in my mind I smile. I smile

from the deep and abiding love I have for you. The memory of you in my mind is something I pray I will carry with me to my grave.

Son, you bring me joy. And for that, I give thanks to God.

Love,

Mom

DAY 86

Christopher-

Wow- Life can be a little crazy, but the thing that normalizes it is the love and care of people that love you, ride for you and hold you down. I hope you are clear that you have people in your life that fit that bill; me included.

I hope your Friday is blessed beyond measure. Keep reaching for greatness...it is in You!!!

Love,

Mom

DAY 87

My beautiful Son, Christopher-

Today, I pause to give immense thanks to God for your life. Though you are choosing separation right now, I can't imagine and don't want to imagine my life without you in it.

You are one of the sources of inspirations that makes me strive so hard to succeed. I always want you to be proud of me and I always want to walk in the earth in a way that leaves a positive legacy for you and Kenny.

Today, I just want you to know how grateful I am that you are part of my life.

Have a Sensational Sunday!!
Love, Mom

DAY 88

Christopher-

Today is a day that is a mixed bag of tricks. First, I am feeling so at peace as I listen to the rain sitting in the chair by the window with the window up. On the other hand, I am exhausted from the past week. Our Chapter of DST took a line and I Spec'd (sponsored) Ms. Shannon (works for I Know I Can), so I had to be all in. My body is super tired, I am having a flare and it hurts all over. Getting old sucks. LOL

I hope you had a great weekend. What's new with you?

How are you really doing? I hope life is treating you well and if it isn't, I hope the tide turns soon. You deserve a good life. I am praying for you daily.

Love,

Mom

DAY 89

Christopher-

Today is my calm day to reminisce about life. I love these days. Reflection always gives me peace. As I get ready for the day, I am reminiscing about all of the things that make me love you so much. As I am typing, I am smiling. This journey with you has been the toughest, but best part of my life. I now understand Grandma so much better than I ever did. I never understood how a woman who did not give birth to me and who saw me at my worst could still love me so much. I now know and believe her love for me. Love is so not about approving of or agreeing with everything one does. It is about choosing to know the worst, but see the best and love...still. It is about praying through the storms, trusting that God will return the sun...again.

Yep, I really do understand what Grandma's real love for me means, cuz that is the same type of love I have for you. Through gun charges, drugs use, tattooed necks, and bouts with self-destruction, I LOVE YOU!! None of that diminishes my deep and abiding love for my Son. In fact, the feelings that emerge through those things really help me to know for myself what real love is and to admit that I have mad, real love for you.

Have a great day, my beautiful, Son-shine!!!

Love, Mom

DAY 90

Christopher-

This morning, I arose with praise in my heart because God has already promised me that He has got you. No matter what the devil wants me to believe, God reminds me daily that He has designated you for the Kingdom of God and that all that you go through now will merely be part of your testimony when you finally say yes to Jesus.

So, today and every day, I give thanks to God for you. I really do believe you are God's special gift to me. When the pain of life feels like it is overwhelming and when you feel as though you can't stop the spiral, just know that your Mom is somewhere praying for you and trusting that God has your back. That knowledge helps me to sleep well and to have peace in the midst of a chaotic world.

Today, keep you head up and call your therapist. :-)

So, have the BEST weekend EVER. I LOVE YOU!

Mom

DAY 91

Christopher–

Today as I was watching my Buckeyes play the first game of the season, I missed your voice screaming, "Let's Go", hearing your door open and hear you ask, "Mom, did you see that play?"

Today feels a little strange cuz I can really feel the sting of missing you. But, I am sure you know that when you are ready, I will be waiting to receive you with open arms, flaws and all.

I thought this card summarized how I feel, cuz you know how

much I love Starbucks, but I have not had it since the boycott began in April. :-)

Have a great rest of your Saturday.

Love,

Mom

DAY 92

Christopher-

I'm sure you are giving me side-eye because I sent a card that said you are awesome!! Well...the fact of the matter is, you are. Your awesomeness isn't about the choices that you make. If that were the case, none of us would ever be awesome. Your awesomeness is based on who you are at your core. The Christopher you never let most people see, because you are afraid they might think you are weak and take advantage of you. But, as your Mom, I know the truth of who you really are.

Yesterday, Aunt Tanya and I were talking about how awesome you really are. She talked about the great memories she has of you and how much she misses you. She talked about your farting contests and how much she loved having you at the house during the summer and how much we miss you guys being young and spending the night on Thanksgiving so we could shop on Black Friday for y'alls Christmas gifts.

I was telling her how much I loved the handmade ornaments you made when you were little and how I always put them on our tree. Then I got sad, cuz it hit me that this will be the first Christmas that we will be apart.

But, I want you happy above all else, so I will just get over myself and let you be happy spending your first Christmas with your other family. Regardless, I wanted to take time today to tell you that I know your heart and I know how AWESOME you really are.

Love,

Mom

DAY 93

(Special Announcement Card)

Christopher-

My announcement is:

I LOVE YOU WITH MY WHOLE HEART...and there is nothing you can do about it!!

When it feels like the world is pooping on your head, open this e-card and take comfort in the knowledge that you have a Mother who loves you and is here to wipe the poop away. :-)

Seriously Son, when you need a shoulder, a listening non-judgmental ear, a caring heart, words of wisdom, sound advice, or someone to hold you in their arms I will always be here for you. That is part of the job description of Mother. Each day and night I pray for you and I pray for Grandma. Each of you hold the dearest parts of my heart and both of you need me now. So, like a true warrior, I am standing strong for both of you.

I love you my beautiful boi.

Mom

DAY 94

Christopher-

I simply wanted to send this card today to simply say, "Thank You" for the gift of hugging you. That made my whole week.

I needed you to see in my eyes what loves looks like. There is no judgement; only love. No matter what you bring to the table, as your Mother, my job is to love you through it.

Have an "Amazing" day my beautiful, outstanding Son.

Love, Mom

DAY 95

Christopher-

You know I don't celebrate halloween, but I still wanted to come on to acknowledge the date and to tell you I hope that whatever you are doing is fun and safe.

When you look in the mirror this weekend, look behind the image that you see, to see the man that you are. He is phenomenal and I hope you never forget that. I know I never forget who you really are. That is all I allow myself to see and believe.

I love you Son. Mom

DAY 96

Christoper-

Today, I am watching Pastor
John Hannah on YouTube as
church. It is a great reminder
to remind you that in the midst
of everything you are going
through and facing, God is with
you. Even when it feels like you
are alone, God is omnipresent
(Everywhere) and he has not
forgotten about you. He is so
patient. HE is waiting for you.
He is not pushy and will never
force you to serve him. He
simply shows up with little
reminders that He is with you.

As much as I love you and am down for you like four flat tires, my love pales in comparison to His great love for you. The seeds of who He is were already planted inside you.

Today, my prayer is that God will send you great comfort and that He covers you with his protection. As I go about me day, I will keep you top of mind and give thanks to God for your life and that He chose you for me.

Love,

Mom

DAY 97

Christopher-

I found this new e-card and I loved it. A couple of weeks ago, Auntie Dionne and I went down to the Hocking Hills so that I could see the beautiful leaves before they all fell from the trees. I love fall because it represents for me a reminder that like nature, our lives have seasons and with each season comes change; some good, some bad. Unlike nature, we have control if change will come with our seasons.

I hope you will avail yourself of the chance and the choice to

change the things in your life
that are not producing the kind
of life you want for yourself. At
some point, allowing
circumstances to zap the life
from you will get old. You
certainly don't want to be the
same person at 20 that you
were at 15. If you are, it is a
clear sign that you are not
evolving into a greater version of
yourself. I know you don't think
that you deserve a great life. I
can tell by the choices that you
make that your internal self
(who you really are) is in conflict
with your external self (who you
pretend to be).

Have you noticed that your
external self has not caused me
to love you any less? Are you

afraid that if your internal self wins the battle, others won't understand, or worse won't love you? If they can't love who you really are, ask yourself, is it really love.

As you continue to battle against yourself, I will be in your corner with a towel and some water, waiting to throw you back into the ring of life. That my Son, is love. "If you lost you can look and you will find me; time after time. If you fall I will catch you, I'll be waiting; time after time."

Love,

Mom

DAY 98

Christopher-

I am sure you are wondering why I chose a "Congratulations" card today. Well...So glad you asked. Yesterday, you took one more important step into manhood. You stepped into a space that makes you uncomfortable, but is so necessary for you to grow as a man. You admitted that you need help/advice. God never intended for life to be lived alone. No person has a good life by doing it alone. Part of the reason God gives kids parents is so that they don't have to navigate life alone.

Just because you are chronologically and technically an adult, doesn't mean that as your Mom, I don't have more to teach you. In fact the part of your brain responsible for decision-making, the frontal lobe, doesn't fully develop in males until about 25. That is why it sometimes is difficult to figure out tough decisions at this stage of life for you. Yep, it's totally normal.

Yesterday, helping you to lay out your options made me feel alive. Indeed, it was in that process that I realized God's continued purpose for my life as your Mom. It is to guide you through decision-making, versus making the decisions for you.

Regardless of the decisions you make, I meant what I said, "I love you," anyway.

Love,

Mom

DAY 99

Christopher–

This card says "Hope turns the caterpillar into a butterfly." I've got a secret; becoming a butterfly is scary. It requires leaving our comfort zones and moving into unchartered territory. Often, that fear is why so many people never reach their apex. It is not a lack of skill, talent or ability. It is fear. In my speeches I often say, "Fear is a dream inhibitor, not a dream enhancer." As I write this to you, I suddenly realize that fear doesn't just inhibit dreams, it literally kills dreams. I think I will start using that phrase so that people will really understand why it is so important to "Face Your Fears."

As you start to come out of your cocoon to face adulthood, do get scared and run back to your comfort zone. You have everything that it takes to be your BEST self. God trusts you with greatness Son.

All of my love (AOML),

Mom

DAY 100

As I write this card, I am reminded of the story of Job. The enemy of our souls kept tempting Job because he thought if he kept taking all of the things Job loved, he would curse God. But, in spite of losing everything, Job never did. He loved and trusted God. Because he didn't stop trusting him, God restored to Job all that the enemy had destroyed.

I have spent the last 5 months telling you how much I love you and that nothing you do will stop my love for you. I have continually told you that my job is not to judge your choices, but to love you through them. As I grapple with your latest decision that will have lifelong consequences for you, my faith in God is being tested. When I learned the news, I asked God, "How much more do you think my heart can take?"

Through tears, I am typing this card to you. This is one of those times that I have to leave this in God's hands. I know that somewhere in the middle of it all is God's plan for your life. So, though I don't really trust you and I am having trouble trusting me, I do trust God.

I think I will take some time to "feel" my way through this. Though these cards might cease, my love for you never will. My heart is broken yet again, but I guess that is a risk I taking for choosing to love you. Though I am sad, if I had to choose to love you all over again, I would still choose you. I am disappointed in your choice, but I am saddened that you didn't tell me. Once again, you let me find out in the streets. Do I mean nothing to you? You say you love me, but love would never let me find out this news "Dad" in the streets. More and more you remind me of my brother. Grandma found out he was married, in the streets.

That broke her heart, cuz like me, she loved him dearly.

Going forward, you don't need to pretend to need my advice. Just tell me what you want/need. You didn't need my advice. You needed me to spot you some funds until your first pay check. That's fine. Just tell me that going forward. No more games Christopher. Just truth.

Today, even in the midst of this pain, still, I feel the compulsion to write to you as I have for the past 5 months. I hope that through these notes, you feel the love that flows through my broken heart.

All of my love,

Mom

There were more than 150 love notes from which to choose. I chose to share 100 of them. I share them with you in their original format, font and context. I changed the color of the font to keep the book affordable. I included some notes that were filled with humor and others that had more serious messages of instruction, hope, joy and most of all love.

My relationship with this son (I have another son) is still strained. He is still making poor choices, but even in the midst of all that I see and all that he does, I continue to love him. I will admit that in this season, it is difficult to demonstrate my love for him because my love is having to swim past layers of emotional scar tissue and decay and is pumping through a broken heart. One thing of which I am assured, God is the mender of broken hearts. He is also a restorer. So, in obedience, I will still write to my son (after I am done sulking) and will gather the energy to love him through all of his choices, because as I often tell him, *Love is a Verb!*

In this season, I am having to grapple with the distinction between mothering a child and mothering an adult. To all of the parents reading this page who are struggling and wondering what I have learned, here it is. When we parent children, we make decisions for them. When we parent adults, we guide them in making their own decisions. When they are children and they make mistakes, we show up to rescue them from their mistakes. When they are adults we come alongside them to support them as they face the consequences of their choices, but we don't rescue them from those consequences. If we don't learn that lesson, we stunt their emotional and developmental growth and will be parenting children, not adults for the rest of our lives.

This is a time where in full transparency, I have to admit that the kind of love God is requiring of me for my son is only possible with God's help. In and of myself the continual breaks in every chamber of my heart would cause hardening of my emotional arteries. But, at every turn, God reminds me of the love that my parents showed me when I was at my worst. Further and more importantly, He reminds me of His great love for me, without condition and without judgement. Those thoughts humble me and bring me back to let my love flow through my broken heart.

All of My Love (AOML),
~The "Amazing" Tei Street